LETTER TO POPE THEODORE

Victor of Carthage,

Bishop of Carthage

Translated by: D.P. Curtin

Dalcassian
Publishing
Company

PHILADELPHIA, PA

ISBN: 978-1-960069-73-3 (Paperback)

Library of Congress Control Number:
Author: Curtin, D.P. (1985-)

Front cover image: Nicholaus II, Österreichische Nationalbibliothek - Austrian National Library
Book design by J.J. Ripplestick

Printed by Ingram Content Group, 1 Ingram Blvd, La Vergne, Tennessee

First printing edition 2020.

Introduction

This letter is from a relatively obscure member of the African church, a certain Victor, who was likely bishop of Carthage later in life. The exact date for this letter is unclear. We only know that Theodore held the papal office during its composition, between the years 642 and 649 AD. Certainly, Theodore I's pontificate struggled with the issue of Monthelitism, particularly with the See of Alexandria. The author mentions a certain 'Paulus' who resides in "the royal city", which is almost certainly Paul II, Patriarch of Constantinople, who had never been recognized by the Roman See for some controversy relating to his predecessor.

The intention of the letter is unclear. Victor asks no questions to Theodore, and he does not report anything that would be considered novel for this time. It appears to be largely an act of submission to papal authority, or rather an assurance of submission. The Eastern Empire's reconquest of north Africa had lead to a number of jurisdictional issues with various bishoprics, and this appears to be clarification of the Pope's role as 'Patriarch of the West'.

D.P. Curtin
February 21, 2020
Glen Mills, PA

Epistle to the most blessed and honorable holy brother Pope Theodore from Victor.

The works and glorious conversation of your most blessed fatherhood, acceptable to God, are evident to almost the whole world. Therefore, while the whole earth is filled with apostolic preachings and doctrines, the culture of the true faith. Yet through the learning of divine discourses, your instructive and great exhortations, the orthodox Church of Christ is built up, founded on the apostolic institution, and most firmly strengthened by the faithful Fathers. To which all the most blessed apostles, endowed with a fraternity of honor and power, turning the ranks of the peoples, piously and sacredly led men from darkness to light, from darkness to the true faith, from death to life.

This was foretold by the grace of divine predestination, with salutary precepts and admonitions. The fraternity of your holy apostles is to be honored, following more fully their merits, and more perfectly fulfilling their examples, adorns the Church of God with honesty of deed and sanctity of action. We are, therefore, to be living in holy faith and good Christian behavior, which God has commanded to be done, working incessantly and completely in our priestly studies, keeping the commandments of that divine law. For 'it is not the hearers of the law who are righteous with God', as the apostle says, but the doers of the law will be justified (Romans 1). In which divine law, along with your holy and venerable sincerity, as it is written, must be meditated upon day and night (Psalm 1). This meditation is not observed only by reading through the figure of letters but abounding in the grace of Christ. It is known in your conscience immovably implanted, in no way departing from your heart the sacred law of Christ the Lord God, as the prophet says in the Psalms: 'The mouth of the just shall meditate wisdom, and his tongue shall speak judgment' (Psalm 36).

God's law is in our own heart: 'written not with ink, but with the spirit of the living God'. Not in tablets of stone, but in the carnal tablets of the heart (2 Corinthians 3), as the letter of the blessed apostle Paul to the Corinthians teaches us. Having said this, we signify to your God-pleasing fraternity that, on the seventeenth day of the fourth indictment of the Augustan calendar, we humbly received the consecration and robe of honor in the holy cathedral church in the city of Carthage. In the height of dignity, we may be ruled by Almighty God from the highest, and freed from evil deeds, priestly not only in name, but by the protecting help of Christ our God. May we have merit, commending ourselves to your holy and acceptable prayers to God, we ask that, inasmuch as we are protected by your supplications poured out for us to God, and equipped with all adroit education, we may become worthy with all of the Christian peoples of the protection of the divine veil entrusted to us.

Therefore, to greet your holy and honorable fraternity, we in turn appointed Mellosus, your humble brother, our bishop, and Redemptus, the deacon, or Crescitus notary of our holy see, your servants, whom we ask to be speedily paid for us by your beatitude, so that they may return to their own churches before the winter, by the grace of God.

Before all I confess that at the very beginning of our progress our heart was not slightly wounded, so that I desired that prophetic precept, saying: 'Who will give water to my head, or a fountain of tears to my eyes, so that I will sit and weep day and night (Jeremiah 9)?' For behold, the churches of God are not lightly disturbed, we do not support the voices of Christians, nor do be heed the groans of the bishops, the novelties of those who complain and cry out, or the figments of conspiracy, approved by our venerable priest Paul, as it is said, must be rejected against the true faith. We, however, having tempered our passions with reasons, thought it expedient to support with equanimity the attainment of our aforesaid blessed priests, and to bring this very thing to the hearing of your venerable fraternity with the most watchful care.

For they say, in a certain turn of epigrams, that rolls of paper were lately hung up in the sacred houses of the royal city, entirely contrary to the Catholic religion, and to the true faith itself, and to the traditions of the Fathers. For who, with a sacrilegious voice, dares to preach that in our Lord Jesus Christ there is either only one will, or only of one operation, while the clearest definitions of the Fathers make it obvious that our Lord Jesus Christ has two natures, and there by two wills, and two operations or natural properties are to be found in all ways. We can, therefore, strengthen the insight into our own humble opinions by the many documents of the Fathers, unless we hold your most holy brotherhood in all hearts to retain them most firmly. In order that we may be confirmed in all things by the decrees of the apostolic see itself, we saw that it contains the definition of the apostolic memory of your most blessed predecessor Leo, which was inserted (Epistle 10).

For each nature acts with the communion of the other which is proper. We, therefore, following the decrees of the Fathers in all things, in Christ our Lord we firmly preach the two natures, and their two wills, and their two operations. We truly confess the true God and the true man without human transgressions, rejecting the falsifications, vanities, and lying madness of all heresies. It is yours, therefore, most holy brother, to meet with canonical discretion what is usually contrary to the Catholic faith, and not to permit it to be said anew that the authority of the venerable Fathers did not at all approve. For we, humble in heart, which are upright and wise with the helper of the Lord, are bound together with you by one bond of charity, strongly defending the true faith and the Catholic religion in all things.

Therefore, to be able to resist more diligently from unscrupulous Catholics, we must be threatened, lest we be oppressed by the torpor of laziness, held liable to the guilt of silence, and judged as if we were hanging favors, while we neglect to repel the adversities of the Catholic faith. For it was said by the blessed Felix the apostle, the predecessor of your sanctity: 'For to neglect, when you can, to disturb the perverse, is nothing else but to encourage'. Nor does he lack the scruple of a secret society, which ceases to meet the manifest criminal.

It is clear, most holy teacher, that the venomous cunning of serpents without simplicity is the deceitful fallacy of heretics. For what is the purpose of taking away the properties of the natures in Christ our Lord, except to introduce a confusion of those same natures? The Catholic Church, embedded in the statutes as much as possible of the Holy Fathers of the Council of Chalcedon, from which the foundation of faith and its perfection undoubtedly consist of. We could, indeed, have directed similar writings to our brother and co-bishop Paulus, the most blessed of the royal city, had we not known of the evils, that it had been said by false expressions that our province, as it were in Africa, was capable of doing evil things which do not consist in the truth. Yet, we also submit this, our request, that those things which were written in the epistle by our co-bishops, from our holy council to the most blessed archbishop Paul, so that you are commanded to direct the same to our brother Paul through the representatives of your beatitude.

LATIN TEXT

Epistola Domino beatissimo et honorabili sancto fratri Theodoro papae Victor.

Vestrae beatissimae paternitatis apud Deum acceptabilis opera et conversatio gloriosa pene mundo toti sunt manifesta. Praedicationibus igitur apostolicis et doctrinis dum verae fidei cultura universa repleta sit terra, per divinorum tamen eruditionem eloquiorum, vestra instruente admonitione exhortatoria, superaedificatur orthodoxa Christi Ecclesia, apostolica institutione fundata, et a fidelibus Patribus firmissime roborata. Ad quam omnes beatissimi apostoli, pari honoris et potestatis consortio praediti, populorum agmina convertentes, pie et sancte de tenebris ad lumen, de lapsu ad veram fidem, de morte ad vitam homines divinae praedestinationis gratia praescitos, salutaribus praeceptis ac monitis perduxerunt. Quorum sanctorum apostolorum vestra fraternitas honoranda sequens plenius merita, et perfectius implens exempla, Ecclesiam Dei morum probitate et actuum sanctitate condecorat, et fide sacra vel Christianis moribus vigens, quae fieri Deo placita praecepit, studiis pontificalibus indesinenter operatur et perficit, servans legis divinae mandata: Quia non legis auditores justi sunt apud Deum, sicut narrat Apostolus, sed factores legis justificabuntur (Rom. I). In qua lege divina vestra sancta et veneranda sinceritas, sicut scriptum est, meditatur die ac nocte (Psalm. I): quae meditatio non lectione per figuram litterarum tantum conspecta, sed uberante in vobis Christi gratia, in vestra cognoscitur conscientia immobiliter insita, nullatenus de vestro corde recedente lege Christi Dei Domini sacrosancta, sicut in Psalmis dicit propheta: Os justi meditabitur sapientiam, et lingua ejus loquetur judicium (Psalm. XXXVI). Lex Dei ejus in corde ipsius: non atramento, sed spiritu Dei vivi vestra in areana conscripta; neque in tabulis lapideis, sed in tabulis cordis carnalibus (II Cor. III), sicut beatissimi apostoli Pauli ad Corinthios missa nos docet epistola. Quibus praemissis, significamus Deo placitae fraternitati vestrae, die decimo septimo Kalendarum Augustarum indictionis quartae, nostram humilitatem divina gratia, suo ut praecepit munere praeveniente, ut vestris sanctis ac Deo dignis precibus, in sancta Carthaginensis civitatis ecclesia pontificalis honoris accepisse consecrationem et stolam. In quo dignitatis fastigio, ut a Deo omnipotente regamur ab altissimo, et a malis actibus liberati, sacerdotale non nomen tantum, sed Christi Domini Dei nostri protegente auxilio, et meritum habeamus, vestris sanctis ac Deo acceptabilibus nos commendantes orationibus, poscimus, quatenus et vestris deprecationibus pro nobis ad Deum effusis muniti, et eruditionibus bonis instructi, digni efficiamur cum omnibus nobis populo Christiano commisso illaesi protegi velamento divino. Ad salutationem ergo vestrae sanctae et honorandae fraternitatis, vice nostra Mellosum humilem vestrum fratrem, nostrum episcopum, et Redemptum diaconum, vel Cresciturum notarium sanctae nostrae sedis, vestros famulos destinavimus, quos postulamus celerius nobis a vestra beatitudine persolvi, quo possint ad proprias ecclesias ante hiemem Deo propitio remeare. Prae omnibus autem fateor, in ipso nostrae provectionis exordio cor nostrum non leviter vulneratum fuisse, ut propheticum illud praeceptum exoptarem, dicens: Quis dabit capiti meo aquam, aut oculis meis fontem lacrymarum, et sedens plorabo die ac nocte (Jer. IX)? Ecce enim ecclesiae Dei non leviter perturbantur, Christianissimorum voces ac gemitus episcoporum non supportamus, querentium et clamantium novitates et concinnationum figmenta, a Paulo venerabili consacerdote nostro, ut dicitur, contra fidem veracissimam approbata debere repelli. Nos autem temperamentum causis innectentes, expedire putavimus, praedictorum beatissimorum consacerdotum nostrorum licet justissimos questus aequanimiter supportare, et ad auditus venerandos fraternitatis vestrae hoc ipsum pervigili cura deducere. Inquiunt enim, quaedam vice epigrammatum, chartarum volumina in sacris aedibus apud regiam civitatem nuper esse suspensa, religioni catholicae et ipsi verae fidei ac Patrum traditionibus omnino contraria. Quis enim vecors sacrilega voce audeat praedicare in Domino nostro Jesu Christo aut unam tantummodo voluntatem, aut unam operationem existere, dum manifestissimis Patrum definitionibus liquidius clareat id Domino nostro Jesu Christo duas naturas, et earum duas voluntates, duasque operationes vel proprietates naturales modis omnibus inveniri? Et possumus multiplicibus Patrum documentis nostrae parvitatis intentionem firmare, nisi vestram sanctissimam fraternitatem in omnibus corde ea retinere firmissime teneamus. Ut autem ipsius sedis apostolicae decretis per omnia confirmemur, Leonis beatissimi praedecessoris vestri apostolicae memoriae definitionem inseri pervidimus, et continet (Epist. X). Agit enim utraque natura cum alterius communione quod proprium est. Nos itaque Patrum in omnibus decreta sequentes, in Christo Domino nostro duas naturas, earumque duas voluntates, duasque operationes firmissime praedicamus, Deum verum atque hominem verum absque delictis humanis veraciter confitemur, repudiantes cunctarum haeresum subsannationes, vanitates et insanias mendaces. Vestrum est itaque, frater sanctissime, canonica discretione solite contrariis catholicae fidei obviare, nec permittere noviter dici quod Patrum venerabilium auctoritas omnino non censuit. Nos enim humiles corde, quae recta sunt adjutore Domino sapientes, uno vinculo charitatis vobiscum sumus constricti, veram fidem ac religionem catholicam in omnibus fortiter defensantes. Studiosius itaque a catholicis improbis posse resistere, imminendum est, ne torpore desidiae oppressi, culpae taciturnitatis teneamur obnoxii, et quasi favorem impendentes judicemur, dum adversa catholicae fidei propulsare negligimus. A beato namque Felice apostolo vestrae sanctitatis praedecessore dictum est: Negligere quippe, cum possis, deturbare perversos, nihil est aliud quam fovere; nec caret scrupulo societatis occultae, qui manifesto facinori desinit obviare. Liquet, doctor sanctissime, venenosa serpentum sine simplicitate astutia, manifesta est dolosa haereticorum fallacia. Quid est enim naturarum in Christo Domino nostro proprietates auferre, nisi earumdem naturarum confusionem inducere? quod catholicae Ecclesiae, id est, statutis quam maxime Patrum sancti Chalcedonensis concilii exstat contrarium, ex quo amplius et fundamentum fidei et perfectio indubitate consistit. Possemus vero etiam eidem fratri et coepiscopo nostro Paulo beatissimo regiae civitatis antistiti similia nostris scriptis dirigere, nisi malorum cognosceremus falsis locutionibus dictum fuisse nostram quasi Africanam provinciam posse aliqua, quae in vero non consistunt, mala peragere. Sed et hoc nostrae postulationi subjungimus, ut ea quae epistolariter a coepiscopis nostris sancti concilii nostri ad beatissimum Paulum patriarcham scripta sunt, per vestrae beatitudinis responsarios eidem fratri nostro Paulo dirigere jubeatis.

The Scriptorium Project is the work of a small group of lay people of various apostolic churches who are interested in the preservation, transmission, and translation of the works of the early and medieval church. Our efforts are to make the works of the church fathers accessible to anyone who might have an interest in Christian antiquities and the theological, philosophical, and moral writings that have become the bedrock of Western Civilization.

To-date, our releases have pulled from the Greek, Syriac, Georgian, Latin, Celtic, Ethiopian, and Coptic traditions of Christianity, and have been pulled from sundry local traditions and languages.

Other Titles and Translations by D.P. Curtin:

First Book of Ethiopian Maccabees (2018)
Protoevangelium of James: Greek and English Texts (2019)
Edicts of the Synod of Paris by Chlothar II, King of Franks (2019)
The Life of St. Desiderius by Sisebut, King of Visigoths (2019)
The Synod of Rome by St. Boniface IV of Rome (2019)
Letter to Pope Theodore by Victor of Carthage (2020)
The Decree of 610 by Gundemar, King of Visigoths (2020)
Laws of the Church by Dagobert I, King of Franks (2020)
The Old Nubian Miracle of St. Mena (2021)
About Fifteen Problems by St. Albertus Magnus (2022)
Testament of Some Former Things by John Scotus Eriugena (2022)
The Georgian Synaxarium (2022)
Instructions: Counsel for Novices by St. Ammonas the Hermit (2022)
The Syriac Menologium and Martyrology (2022)
Book on Religious Exercise and Quiet by St. Isaiah the Solitary (2022)
Vision of Theophilus by St. Cyril of Alexandria (2022)
On Fate (De Fato) by St. Albertus Magnus (2023)
Fragments of 'Chronicle' by Hippolytus of Thebes (2023)
Life of the Blessed Theotokos by Epiphanius Monachus (2023)
Syriac Life of John the Baptist by Serapion the Presbyter (2023)
Second Book of Ethiopian Maccabees (2023)

www.ingramcontent.com/pod-product-compliance
Lightning Source LLC
Chambersburg PA
CBHW070958120626
46546CB00004B/1684